The Inquest of Mind and Matter

Subramanya Rama Rao

ISBN   979-8-88530-465-8

The Inquest of Mind and Matter

I dedicate this book to those wonderful people I have met, sharing their magical influence, love and affection that was truly infinite; and to those clusters of people who bewildered and bewitched me with their margins of insanity.

Subramanya
Rama Rao.

Introduction

Mind is a complex space where thoughts evolve, take birth and expand. Understanding the way the mind functions requires a subtle and sensitive approach.

Reclaiming the missing threads and to develop through self examination. It becomes an essential part of our existence to acquire a sound mind and body.

The psychology of human behaviour is complex and deserves a closer exploration in comprehending the nature of people.

We are unique in our mental make-up and at times incomprehensible, complicated and are complex. Our culture, upbringing and perceptions encompasses our predispositions, prejudices and conditional overhaul.

The influence affects a certain configuration of thoughts that prompts our actions and reactions.

We must agree to believe, human nature is an elusive and ingenious force, cunningly crafted to match individual ordinances of different hues and colours.

Inhabiting this planet, we share resources and live in a cohesive modern society, we need all the nitty-gritty of survival techniques to complete our life cycle.

Man subjugates himself to be a victim of circumstances, during stressful

Intervals behaviour may run chaotic and appear alien, morbid tendencies arise out of strong and emotional moments and a distinct need to undergo a personality change, may look imminent.

Scientists, heart specialists, neuroscientists do agree that emotional upheavals during very stressful periods, such as having to cope up with the loss of a loved one, financial difficulties alters the state of heart, brain pathology and weakens them and their functionality's relationships and mental behaviour. The brain structural changes seen in schizophrenic patients.

At times, mental disposition and the propensity to

cruel and harmful intent towards other people mitigates and aggravates harmful conditions.

The human brain is capable of tuning itself to a robust degree of intellectual standing, traversing all impediments and overcoming barriers.

When we stand consciously close to subtle awareness and introspection, we can seriously contemplate an altered state of mind with no attrition.

Most of our relationship conflicts arises from the practice of discrimination, obsessive indulgence in seeking comfort for the self ends, discording all considerations and lacking of empathy towards other people. Some take it as their birthright and totally confine themselves to self gratification at any cost, and vehemently pursue their evil intentions.

We could use the technique of auto-suggestion, to correct our thoughts and derive favourable benefits. Creating a mental barrier and fix limitations.

We should not despair and continue with remorse when we can change and equip ourselves competently and accept a healthy way of life.

One thing is certain, our intellect and the progression of sound mind and sound body becomes essentially a crying necessity. If we are not open for change we are closing the gates of happiness forever. There is an element of truth and discipline for all of us to make our lives lovable, liveable and sustainable. It calls for a mindset to change, adopt and accept certain realities of life.

Bad behaviour, cunning intelligence, selfishness is a complex deteriorating attitude which cannot go hidden, because it is easily identifiable and noticeable. The complacency attached to this syndrome is unwarranted, the reason being that people with special abilities can see through it.

This compendium of my random thoughts in this book is therefore a study of human behaviour and is centered on psychological approach, permutations and combinations of thoughts, and an inquest as to how subjects reveal themselves. How the mind functions and the complexities arising out of interventions, finding answers to such daunting questions.

It is a stupendous task even to imagine a holistic approach in an attempt to heal the mind, achieving a justifiable level of balance and control, aiming for happier human relationships.

We have become a race too complicated in modern society, we are chasing everything too fast, and never seem to be getting what we want. We have to relearn and understand ourselves from the roots.

In a spiritual sense, the need of the hour, is understanding love and to develop a subtle awareness, as to what love can do in our lives which makes all those healthy differences. In the absence of love, everything turns out to be chaotic.

These random thoughts have originated by intense focus and keener observations, inferences and the varied reactions about how we operate and assert ourselves. Also, this is a long stretched effort in exposing human nature and behaviour as it functions, aspiring a healthier state of a truly well rounded personality.

We have become a race of misguided bravado's pursuing growth too fast laterally, despite the choices of goodness open to us, and have embraced negative energies, in the guise of selfishness, greed and competition.

Preface

To acquire a sound mind and body, we do not have to access high intellectual content and seek the help of ivory tower philosophers. I strongly believe that there are no - art of living techniques and inner engineering treatments to lead a wonderful life of happiness.

If we can practice and adopt a discipline of self-awareness and introspection, it is adequate to rectify our deficits in our personality.

We can judiciously clarify questions to ourselves, seek solutions within the scope of our intelligence, with empathy, unconditional boundaries and find appropriate behavioural, attitudinal responses.

The power of the mind is adequately rooted in our lives, and the faculties of logic sufficiently infused, it is more than adequate to revamp a chaotic mind, starved for a definite tranquil space.

We all suffer from wrong configurations, deficiencies and shortcomings of mind and hardly make any attempt to introspect and reformat our makeup. We can learn to observe, study tendencies and imbibe values enormously.

This book therefore is an attempt to understand and invigorate our intellectual thought process, to bring about a healthy state of mind. This compilation of thoughts reflects how our mind behaves, which exposes its multifaceted dimensions. The inquest is nowhere near saintly perfection nor intended to make it sound like a gospel.

The thought flow is adequate and leaves you at a tangential level and the scope to surmise your own conclusions are very much inviting. An inquest of the mind and the way it responds is deftly studied, given priority and without being judgemental. Thoughts that have stemmed out from this exercise have emerged contextually, and by a certain anguish over inescapable situations. Largely with an aspiring philosophy seeking an ideal state of human relationships.

It appears that we suffer inordinately and repeatedly in an entangled quagmire and struggle aimlessly without direction. Running into a pivotal destiny in a repeat life and death cycle.

In a balanced life, we discord all negativity, our mind relaxes and becomes fully composed, reaching a happier state of mind, prepared to transcend to higher realms of existence.

We need to carry with us this state of peace and tranquillity only to circumvent a coming back of a chaotic life and existence.

The inquest of - Mind & Matter

When you dislike someone for a reason, Your chemistry inwardly changes so much that you can never mold yourself to your original state again.

In our success, we feel an invisible power surging, in failures we realise that the same power is unwilling for an unknown reason denying us the break, destiny is unpredictable.

Life is inundated with fear, anxiety and turmoil. The nature of our existence is impermanence, rekindling the light of joyful living depends on equanimity of our state of mind.

Why do we struggle to make our life permanent, when life in reality is impermanent? Never crave for more than you get, Disown mental poverty and live in peace.

Uncertain relationships work best, when it is operated at intervals, on a switch on and switch off modes, for it serves for the time you serve for such a relationship, some relationships also become a lifetime of pleasant experience and ties you to a human bondage.

Few minutes spent in laughter, joy and understanding with good people is worth a lifetime of happiness, rather than an entire lifetime of vengeance, we pursue with pride and prejudice.

The reason to live gets strengthened by pleasant memories like the time we spend with a child, with loving people around, and the pristine love housing us. We feel wanted and a true sense of belonging surrounds us. What more reasons can one visualise for being happy?

I am a theist, big bang theories do not convince me. It's humanly impossible to believe that life is an accident and a mere coincidence or a freakish happening and knowing that all the life sustaining elements support us by mere chance.

$$W$$hen you reserve time for yourself, you realise what your soul needs, serve it with all the care in the world. Whatever you had denied by giving it, You serve justice for yourself.

All living forms righteously, have their own space and respect ungrudgingly for no creation is undesirable, they come with defined values. Never to devalue and undervalue.

Intervals of misfortune are moments of reawakening. Speed breakers stop pushing us to reality and for introspection, and for true management of our existence, God will handhold and lift us if we realise this truth.

One single act of sacrilege is enough to destroy a whole monumental structure built, we must treat everything with respect, preserve and add value. The value of a thing is known only when it is lost.

When you possess a wicked attitude, you become wretched unknowingly, missing out on finer qualities of loving and compassion. Nurture a happier state of mind for yourself and do not deny yourself what life can give back and accept misery.

When a child shows up with exemplary behaviour, it is surely a character acquired from the previous births, and the good karma accumulates giving them a sound mind. People live long, yet they cannot reform and correct their polluted minds.

I have heard too much about compassion and forgiveness, but I can never forgive people who have caused me pain, for it becomes an unforgettable memory, haunting and hovering above me, to seek peace and to heal I distance myself till the memory becomes extinct.

Conflict arises when we fight for ideologies. We must create our own sphere of space, not to plant anything of ours in other's boundaries. The soil will not be fertile and ideologies get buried.

It looks like God wanted our lives to be a transient one. Created us with a purpose. Birth and death are all a design premeditatively thought, otherwise, all evil inventory built will engulf and suffocate this planet

When we trust God we appreciate life better, become more poignant and expand our horizons.

In silence you realise the truth,
by listening you reach minds,
in seeing you believe, by your actions
you touch souls, become fair to others
and enrich yourself, and you won't lose
anything.

Testing moments must not steal our confidence, and push us to an emotional turmoil. Construe it as a moment of challenge and stand up to the circumstances.

Heightened innocence, time serving affection, gainful participation, support for returns, are the mark of a cunning, crafty mind. Beware of such people and identify them as subservient foes.

By nature human beings cannot contain harsh predicaments, Whatever be their position and valour, their nerves break down. It is in these moments of weakness, the power of prayer seems inevitable. God has to intervene at times!

A true worshiper has nothing to fear, nothing to lose and nothing to regret. God becomes the heart and soul of his being.

C ircumstantial wrong doings appear as if inevitable things carried on in pure self defense, intentional and premeditated actions appear to be an assault on truth, to avoid what is inhuman, it is desired to make our minds as chaste as possible.

Karma doesn't show mercy even to newborn's, it makes them cry in pain, hunger and for security, only to be silent when mother's pick them up! Which is the beginning. God must be merciful.

G od wants to promote good souls, hence he snatches them away early, for others he extends a bit longer time, so they can realize that rewards do not come easy.

Nature somehow reimburse us in the same way we treat others. Selfishness to deprived conditions, good deeds to surprise gifts, for being kind to others to miraculous outcomes. Good deeds invariably come back to us.

When you respect people, you add value to their lives, infuse confidence, and strengthen their morale. The greatest deed one can do is to support someone who has fallen to raise.

If you think by chasing money, you get richer. It may surprise you! Somethings in our destiny harshly teaches us and mould's us differently. Things that money can't buy are health and happiness.

Spiritual strength means; ability to operate in the pristine glory of a pure mind, liberated and being in faith. It's a divine experience.

It is not what destiny gave you,
and you lived. Destiny is merely
a program you have lived. If you truly
deserve better, there are higher portals
of existence. Reaching them is arduous,
but, you have to pursue that wonderful
engagement.

The dead always remind what you could have given, and what you denied them. If you have done your best in their time you have served them well. If you have done within your means, it is a mark that no one can ever erase, not even the dead.

The origin of thoughts is the result of a combination of finer elements, generated through different births in different avatars it cannot be conditioned, it is fluid and conceived, capable for change.

Even by chance if thoughts appear conditioned, the subconscious intervention (the intellect) liberates conditional thinking. The subconsciousness stands aloof and watches the mind.

Hope keeps us alive, faith reassures us, the vision of God and his invisible help is enough to live and prolong life.

N ever take life as if you own it, never be arrogant, you never know when the forces of life can humble you down, lessons learnt in humility have lasting values.

Only total surrender, unflinching faith can take us nearer to God, at times of great misfortune, when we can do nothing! When our limitations are understood.

One should never thwart the favors that destiny gives, allow the sunshine to fall inside your house in gratitude. Because, you will have earned it! It comes to you as a reward.

There exists an incomprehensible bond that sprouts instantly when we meet someone, it is certainly not of the present! Relationships are of the past and it attracts or repels instantly.

Never leave elderly folks empty, fill them with love and joy whatever ways. Not because they are unfulfilled, but because they will have given you everything that they have possessed and will be looking for love.

Something is lost, something is gained in life, when the term ends we leave behind whatever that was lost and gained in this transition cycle. What remains in memory is how much we gave and made others happy in our lifetime.

The mind must practice detachment, like the raindrops falling on green grass, unattached and yet not belonging, clear and transparent. Belonging to everything, but distanced. Attachments cause pain, detachment balances both the good and the bad.

When we fall, we realize the depth. When we fly, the sky shows the limit. When we walk we know our health, when can we realize God in a lifetime of struggle, pain and sufferings?

We use just a fraction of our life to love others, we become obsessed with the self, lose out on time to heal ourselves by not loving others, we disregard the power of love.

When you are blessed and receive love from senior people, some mystical force shields you in your most difficult times. The protection secures you when all attempts deployed would have failed and you find no explanation for being protected.

The more you eliminate undesirable relationships, the more you find peace within, with no plans to harm or heartbreak and finding space inside the cocoon to heal!

Acts of kindness will not cost you anything, but to spare it, many people take a step back not to commit to others' difficulties, they think it is an enormous burden. Kindness must come within without any compulsions.

A person who desires to be in the forefront always, talks of himself alone and forces others to talk about him, drawing onto himself all the attention by others is the one who wants the whole world to serve him, discarding others. Such people are blindly obsessed with self.

Birth doesn't determine success or failures in our life, it's a lone battle to survive an unknown destiny, which is slated for all of us to complete. It is an opportunity to lead a wonderful life, a gift from God.

Families do not prevail merely by living together, the circle of love and respect must be shared in togetherness to complete it. In the absence of love, living together for security, will crumble down without the right pillar's support.

The moment you laugh at yourself, admit mistakes, show the world what you are without having to wear masks, no hide and seek, you truly start living well. Nobody is born perfect.

By disowning families, we discord the scope of living together, miss out on greater bondage of love, denying ourselves that wonderful growing years, loving childhood for our children and in the process, we die a lonesome death. In our death even the crows hesitate to sit on our graves.

Sometimes, doing good to others may appear thankless, let us do it for our own sake, mental health, wellbeing and rejuvenation. When you share the spirit of goodness, universal love surrounds us.

Belief - that God is within you, by itself proves a superior strength, a certainty, that no evil can challenge you! It empowers you to face and resist any negative circumstances and challenges in life.

Gaining what you want, by discord and neglect of others priorities, makes you realize that the gain you derived won't stay for long. Things you acquire by the good wishes of others, goes a long way, than snatching it all in selfishness.

Never belittle the life you lived, the life path you had chosen, having lived long enough to complete it. The value of the struggle, successes and failures is the price we all have to pay in our lifetime and for challenges we confront.

I feel God's presence beside me always, earthly existence rolls on its own accord completing its chores, daily routines day after day, it becomes essential to conserve our mental strengths and confidence in a spiritual way to succeed.

Never steal individual liberty, it is the identity of the soul, ego, respect and honour we all have to respect. Give them the honour they deserve. And never undermine them in public. Treat them like the way you want them to treat you.

The presence of a loving soul, enlivens the whole atmosphere to sparkle, whereas the loveless, eclipses the Sun to darkness. The forces of a positive person impact others around.

Life won't promise us anything, it sweeps us by its tides, takes us to uncharted seas, we have to find a boat and paddle our way to our destination.

Faith in God keeps us alive, Prayer strengthens and invigorates us. If we step out of it, the whole eternity becomes a vertigo experience. Mankind has no alternatives and sustainability, his limitations are a mute testimony.

A healthy mind and a healthy attitude are sustainable energies, we must constantly endeavour to stimulate it and carry it wherever we go, to heaven or hell. Attitudes fortify our personalities.

If people respect you, reciprocate. If they don't, you respect them nonetheless. They represent their behaviour, you represent yours.

A good doctor takes the role of a God, proves himself a saviour, and relieves pain, suffering and cures. I always feel I am compensating him less, my gratitude and compensation appears inadequate.

Life's issues are best dealt with pragmatism, the emotional approach aggravates and sets panic, which is undesirable.

There is a streak of pleasant destiny in all our lives, that favours us unconditionally, falling onto our lap and sweeps through us lifting our misery and grief. This is ordained by God's grace alone.

How soothing it is when we think of God almighty in our final hours of departure. Faith is reassuring! If we have none, it's a misfortune!

We easily compare our load of karma with that of others burdens, and punish ourselves. We need to see how much we have overcome rather than seeing how much we are still carrying.

When the mind is focused on the divine, in turbulent times beseech God, some incomprehensible pathways stretch in front of us as if we are planted on the ground to grow and blossom.

Philosophy is an elixir for the mind, when you can do nothing to change people, circumstances and setbacks of life, the easiest way out is to become a philosopher. This is a universal healing technique which holds the entire cosmic energy!

The best way to lift yourself from depression is to give yourself space and time, filled with love and respect to bounce back in life. God has created you for a purpose, empowered you, you are your own master. No force can stop you.

Once upon a time...nature, birds, animals, seas...were in its pristine form, untouched and not desecrated! Mankind has destroyed everything God has gifted. Now what is left is inundated with dust, filth and stench. Our gift for the younger generation.

A beautiful mind is sensitive to others as much as it cares for itself, taking care of others gently, being receptive and having respect for others.

Without reverence for nature and its rightful place on earth, we are just zombies existing in a barren land. Protect and preserve nature in gratitude, so it can protect us.

God doesn't interfere in our karmas, we cannot over burden him and drag him down to our advantages. If we deserve to be uplifted we have to pray for him. He may give us sustaining power to finish our assigned labour.

Imposing intellectual thoughts may derail the masses. It is better to cascade it down slowly with fluidity for a touch and gliding it away!

A good man introspects his past, his present, and the future, and life differentiates, buries and mourns them all, for it teaches nothing and leads him to nowhere, it is his destiny that he lived and survived.

When you burden everything on others, yet blame their faltering steps, you are unfair, selfish and uncaring, take a portion of their pain and know what they struggle for.

When you willfully hurt someone, you shame your birth as an individual, the consequence of subjecting others to persecution of some sort, this can rebound in the same greater force and hurt you even more, every action both good and bad brings a reciprocal effect.

A person who upholds all your actions, with you in your times of glory, sharing joy will be the first to walk out on you, in your times of hardships. Assuredly, he was there with you for some returns.

The real sense of loss is knowing that you cannot setright the circumstances, change the time and the place, which you have undone wantonly by ignorance or arrogance.

You can never expect miracles from a defective mind, even prayers cannot reach the labyrinth of expectations. Miracles can only happen when you have purity of mind and praying faith.

The mind is everything, it is a laboratory that can create happiness and unhappiness. Understand it's mechanism. Keep it healthy and buoyant.

When misfortunes strike you, somewhere a blade of grass swings in your favour offering you hope, assuring hope telling you that you are not alone. When you look up to your circumstances it may predict a promising better future. Trust God and never lose faith in him.

Compulsive narcissism is an inherent sickness, it separates, denigrates personal integrity and character. When life backfires on you, you may not have strength even to stand on your legs.

We think we are immortals, wanting everything, more than what we get and find happiness in possessions, pushing others priorities and grabbing what belongs to them, living sadistically. Truth is, nothing belongs to you forever and you cannot own anything that is not yours.

All things change, circumstances and relationships. But if you allow kindness and love to mature in the place, you create a happier world.

I gnorance and greed do not bring
happiness. It gives a euphoric
sense of gratification. But It soon shows
the futility of the action it can play.

L ife samples us everything in bits and pieces, proud moments, depressing times, even giving spoils of war, yet we colour everything and live ostentatiously!

As if life's challenges are not enough, our seat of memory continuously heaps heavier loads on our hunchbacks. Human existence has never been comfortable to anyone.

Sometimes. Even to take what is truly yours. You have to sacrifice a lot. For others can be there to snatch with no guilt and conscience.

There comes a time. When you have to disown everything that has caused you pain. Shrink the world to your size to find peace.

When you lose something, don't cry for it, it simply means that it didn't belong to you. If it was truly yours, you would never have lost.

Corrupt people certainly like the good Samaritans, because they miss out on all decent morals so much, they desire very much to be in respectable association. So they can promote themselves, making their status look good.

When you come to realise that your loved ones are not treating you important, and they forget what you did to them, you live with the memories of what you did for them, and become a philosopher.

Behind every rudeness, ill-temper, and greed lies a past disquiet. Unless we mutate for better by introspection. Not every setback in life can impact our psyche! We are a much stronger species, who can resist evil.

Learn from the wisdom of ages, truth cannot be reinvented, it can be discovered. Foolish mind alone neglects it. No society can ever say.

If God gives us a second chance to relive our lives, everything being the same, how many of us would take it?

Destiny is a path that drags you to it's circle, notwithstanding your best of plans, struggles and ability to overcome. Free- will is uncertain in it's own ways! It doesn't operate the way we anticipate.

How did God fit us into this beautiful world? We lack even a reasonable character, ability to retain what he has given us? Some eternal gifts of nature need to be protected with a great sense of humility and indebtedness.

Silence can be deafening, silence can be a blessing and silence can unjustifiably be mute and careless. We can use this tool of silence in any way we choose either for war or peace.

Childhood is best remembered for love, adolescence for understanding, adulthood for the mercy of God, old age for compassion. Our lives would be a paradise experience if we amassed all these blessings.

The amount of joyful experience I received is proportional to the love that I have given to others, moments of joy I have created for others, and the laughter I induced for others.

Prayers of an impure mind are unheard, prayers of a stable mind are heard. God responds only for the discerning! God cannot be dragged for all intentions.

The root cause of all emotional suffering is due to those things we want to hide, calling it too personal. We are liberated the day we deport it.

Old values must be studied with new perspectives, imbibed in our lives, without discord and bias, old and new both carry great values in the right protocols.

Bitterness and animosity if pursued can weaken the very moral fibre and render us to monstrous behaviour. We must purge out all forms of animosity. Cleans our mind

$\mathbf{B}$e cautious when you judge people, you know not the circumstances that changes a good person to act erratically. Life is not a hammock to sleep and swing in drowsiness.

A non believer, is one who finds comfort in his thoughts and disbelieves in every limitation, of his intelligence, existence of the cosmos and thinks that all life sustaining elements and nature evolved only to support him.

Knowledge lights up life in more ways than one, ignorance isn't bliss, it desecrates a superior birth. Intellect compliments good life.

The gentle way to address an insult, is to make the person who insulted you to witness a large crowd, giving you a standing ovation and applause!

Spending more time with children, and making them happy, and cheerful, we come under a spell, by those tiny precursors of life who can infuse true character in us. Lessening our stressful life. They are harbingers of innocence and are divine angels.

Never set boundaries for love, from physical to spiritual forms, if love can make you purest, without blemish and tinted colours, it can expand exponentially and grow limitless.

When we vehemently pursue perceived happiness, with greed and selfishness, nature plays a role to teach us where we have gone wrong? in a subtle way!

Time spent in introspection and dissension of bad behaviour and fixing it, assures us a good life by choice. The more we dig into our inner matrix we will be able to find corrosion-resistant areas we can sterilize. Racing against time, be conscious of things to discontinue and optimize, or you may have surprises!

$$\mathbf{R}$$eptilian nature in men can never be underestimated, their agility, reflexes and skills of trapping their prey is unmatched. Their instincts will remain the same. Never take them for confidence.

Our birth is predestined, programmed and is handed over to us. Inescapable game play to win or to lose, play it well and leave behind a history of love, and a conscious surrender to almighty God.

Death of a loved one appears to be more tragic and inconsolable at a personal level, the external world may look uncaring and insensitive to our misfortune. It adds bitterness by ticking away the same world in oblivion as if it doesn't care a damn.

The world must contain good values, justice, kindness and love in abundance and must not perish from the face of this planet.

For some people we become an object of hate, dislike and discord, it's a natural selection. For some we become objects of desire and compassion! People choose what they want and what they are looking for.

Attitudes are an inner reflection of the mind, some are conditioned, some are liberated, it's the passion that craves with an endless pursuit to fulfil its hunger. Obviously, it is the mind that needs enlightenment.

Almighty, gave us bountiful resources, food, water, oxygen on earth for existence but, seems to have forgotten giving us peace of mind, happiness, and perhaps wished that we could earn all that by ourselves. I think he made a mistake.

The best moments in life are those, when we have made elderly folks smile, given love and affection, not looking for any kind of returns. Treating them with respect and sharing laughter.

When you take care, serve humanity, filling a need and wiping a tear, for the discerning you appear as God incarnate. True humanity is a collective term, all humans put together.

Money can give us a pseudo belief that we can own anything, till such time it tells us that it is useless!

The bird knows that he is tiny
and is trusting God for his life;
man knows he is intelligent and his ego
makes him a nonbeliever!

When the good is transient we are melancholic, when the bad is transient we are relieved. If both become permanent we are disabled!

Good people, in bad circumstances are not condemned to suffering; they are so blessed you find them sparkling next season!

The expanding and limitless scope of science and technology, leaves us always hungry and to be humble. The universe by its vastness and many possibilities makes us feel like small children.

Life is a game play of diminishing returns, as our expectations do not stop but expand, upgrades do not ensure happiness, we must first learn to be happy in what we have!

To better our circumstances we preach positivity, fluidity in testing periods than being reticent. If we go against the current it makes us remorse too, the best of minds are detached both ways, just go alongside.

Continued assault on nature,
results in a pay back causing
distress and devastation, we know only
when it strikes!

Some show such dereliction towards your decent concern, they make it look like ; it is your capacity which is deficient!

S ome traits see a lonesome death.
Attitude, pride and prejudice so
on, have corroded by us so much that
even angels would hesitate to touch us!

Never respond to arrogance, immaturity, and cunningness shown by others, weaken it by your deafening silence, down play the situations as if it has not influenced you. Your strength of character must be firm.

All that belongs to a sick mind is abuse, pride and sadism. They are cursed eternally and don't heal, never attempt to change them!

The value of a thing is known only when it is lost. We neither can replace it nor can we rehabilitate.

The world gives us different choices to be happy, it's our Karma that selects the choices and it makes sure of what we really deserve. It's like what we sow, so we reap. We are rewarded and reprimanded as we deserve.

Tendency of Insecure people is to secure a good life by any means: hook or crook, respect or by disrespect. It pushes them back to horrendous trouble anyways. All good things have to be earned wisely, there are no shortcuts, a certain price has to be paid, so it can stay.

When we find no reason to impress others, live in peace, no ostentatious pretentiousness, laugh at our own mistakes, we have moved towards enlightenment and maturity of mind.

As if to tease and mock at our misfortune, life gives us a chance to claim a mountain when our legs are weak and an opportunity to cross a molehill, when our legs are strong,

Imploring help from a cosmic force doesn't make us smaller; rather, our mindset expands to accept the gifts of providence in gratitude.

Music.. is a transcending wave, a portal that creates other dimensions, to reach an inexhaustible universe!

"Look at the world through the eyes of the poor" fill their needs the best way you can, humanity must never become impoverished and underprivileged. We cannot allow mankind to go begging and impoverished.

Death alone can convince us of impermanence. But we live as immortals as long as we can in this fleeting time warp. With our greed, selfishness and pride.

The games people play in real life, leaves them in an altered state of sickness permanently, changing their brain chemistry in such a way that they never return to their original cellular state.

The soul tells me a loftier message, to become a saint. Virtual life makes me an existential fool in defence of a pseudo-life!

No matter what catastrophe caused the numbness, reinvigorate by a stronger will to survive. Allow the intensity of suffering to pass through you not trying to stop.

Intellect is superior to all the wealth in the world. If you are starved for a beautiful mind, and have tons of wealth, you are still impoverished.

The 'I' generates 'Ego'... which destroys the whole being. It can break families, nations, trigger wars and render us to ashes.

If you cannot survive good people, you have to survive yourself. Rediscover your life, redesign and introspect, and navigate further. By losing good people you dry up much early.

To walk away – from a purposeless, unreasonable situation is perhaps the best alternative left for a matured person. Without taking part in unpleasantness..

God knows all that happens in our lives. Our trust must be unwavering in him. Except that we must stand before him with folded hands!

'Relationships' thrives on mutual respect, trust and love, tolerance and good temper. No one can demean, undermine another and claim supremacy. Through the eyes of God, all are equal.

When you see a rainbow..you see vibrant colours, life also has hues, shades of sorrow and misery, one cannot whitewash it! It fades away on it's own when we have paid it's due.

S ome inflict harm, and make it look like others are sinner's. They are mystically wretched and congenitally pathetic. They are the men who have no conscience. One should avoid such people like a virus..

If money can buy everything, we would further be blind not to differentiate between darkness from light! We may start a new life in darkness.

The best years are spent in childhood, too young for expectations, just innocence, frolics and contended with small gifts of love. It is here that lies the true sense of happiness.

If I ever have looked a bit different, and found lonesome, gentle and reserved; I would surely be in the wrong company, catching my breath looking at wider horizons.

Our conscience alone knows who we are, the rest of it is all about a mask we wear in our lifetime, for a pretentious life.

If I have failed to see the value of a smile on the face of an innocent child, the affection our parents have given, the joy of sharing and living together in the family..what good is all the wealth I have gained in my life? I have missed irrevocable moments.

At times, the spiritual world helps you in your tiresome karma. Whatever good you will have earned are the blessings of elders, whom you have given love and affection. The time you serve your parents is perhaps the best. It's the roots that hold you firmly, enriched by strength and divinity.

When someone is in your obligation, never exploit their circumstances with unconscionable intent, it is like not showing mercy for a bleeding goat in a slaughterhouse.

Sometimes even misfortune is a blessing in disguise. It's God's wish, sudden correction, change of paths we are crossing, His devious ways of working for you are mysterious, which you never know!

If you focus on the hurt, you will continue to suffer. If you mull over it in time it corrodes you, if you persuade, your health deteriorates. We must forget the hurt and start living afresh.

As long as we allow our self
interests to thrive and be
greedy, so long our tears of suffering will
not be over. We must become selfless
and help others and spiritually expand
our intellect.

Those who are lost in an effort of acquiring wealth and cling to it for survival, having convinced themselves that this is the only way for a happier life, will never detach themselves, rest assured, that these people would aspire for a second birth only to retain their wealth.

There is always an underlying truth, that relationships flourish only in mutual interests or it becomes toxic for both. There is always a certain give and take, for any relationship to thrive.

It is impossible to remain a gentleman when sporadically you are being confronted by deceit, cunningness and malice, your defences against these onslaught would touch the very threshold of self defence.

Never overpower people by your wealth, because it isn't permanent, or use it like a commodity to trade, it may slip between your fingers by dawn and drown you by dusk.

God is a supreme artist, he has coloured all pulsating life forms and has created the universe with profound love. If we do not return his love by supporting life, we are at crossroads and fail on our part to undertake the right survival path.

If you refuse to learn lessons from life and nature, and live in pride, your karma alone teaches you in compelling ways.

In the face of misfortune and deprivation, some people who merely witness and escape moral responsibility are not human. Such cowardice and escapist tendencies are most unbecoming.

If you run, you will be bitten by the dog. If you stand still without fear, it stops barking at you! Like so, never run away from a crisis, when you face challenges without fear it gets dissipated.

$$W$$hen you withhold love for the fear of commitment, you stop a precious moment of sacredness and paint the world for the demons to enter.

Enlightened souls look up to God for support even in the good times and in the worst of circumstances. Both the good and the bad are phases we humans have to live with, we overcome by faith alone.

Good relationships must serve all times, the one that stays a while serves just one person, extended ones are for life.

Taking time to appreciate one's own life, by its limitations, dimensions and scope, showing gratitude to God, we receive in excess. The more we expect in greed we come to lose. Being modest and humble, we become richer, happier and mature intellectually.

If you don't stand up to those who ill-treat you, you become a coward beyond repair and allow them to get away, you will then be responsible to breed an uncouth community of perverts.

Choose to live your life as it presents itself, never attempt to run it the way you want, you have no hold on it. It is like diverting tornados and misleading it's path.

Love is an elixir of life for all unfortunate human predicaments. We replace it only with our shades of pride, prejudice and selfishness!

It takes several beatings on red hot iron to evolve a perfect sword, and several wounds for a pristine character. The wisdom comes by suffering and agony, lessons that are learnt the hard way.

An upright person thanks others for their time, considerations and concerns shown towards him. Acknowledging them with gratitude. Some take the benefits and pretend that they owe nothing, nothing to reciprocate and give back, they are insensitive.

The most repulsive behaviour is when people make you miserable and never express a word of regret. They are sadistic and think they have won the race. Never entertain such people.

The more I understand clever people, the more I distance myself. Their chemistry burns my skin. They are the ones who claim to be intelligent and continue with their sick mind. They are shamelessly arrogant.

A conceited mind can be seen
even in the darkest hours, or
seen amidst a gathering, and their faces
can tell you a hundred stories! It takes a
keen sense of observation and didactic
talent.

The chemistry of relationships is so complex, fluid and unpredictable it can never be constant. Acceptance, rejection revolves in a never-ending cycle, if it is very complex do not strain to understand. Leave it alone.

Hibernate like a polar bear in tough times, when the weather is good, step out to fight out, never suffer emotionally. Emotional turmoil is more devastatingly harmful than the sickness itself.

We all have to carry our baggage without regrets, the more we complain, the heavier it becomes. Till you cannot take the karmic load any more.

Being pious does not mean you reject the unholy, it's only when you experience the bad you truly appreciate the good.

There is a certain melancholia in our lives, taken at the lead, that can paint the world into an angry red planet. Human kind must create happiness, rekindle joyous living from moment to moment, and celebrate our existence.

There are many times in life one has to lie and get away with lies, these are used for self defense and also to protect another. Truth has many faces and are not the same, truth cannot be constant, it has to be found from moment to moment.

What we discovered is just a pebble on the beach, what remains to be explored is unfathomable in the universe.

Unreasonable people are entrenched in an imperfect world so much that if they are found missing, the world looks impossibly perfect!

Never deny the needs of aged parents, by giving and fulfilling their needs, the satisfaction we derive will be immense, and totally enlivens us for life.

Never hate, dislike or be unreasonable to others, to make a difference, disown your negativity. Extend unconditional love. Disassociate from what likely discomforts you.

Difficult people, trouble others expecting others' sanity, they expect others to be forgiving and want to be treated with respect and kindness. Their morbid selfishness compels them even to ask from others what they are not capable of giving.

All that you acquired by craftiness, and selfishness, exploiting others, can never stay with you. You have got it by the rolling stone freakishly, which never gathered mass and you lose it.

From the roots a stem, branch and a leaf takes birth, these living forms continue to get nutrition and water from the roots symbiotically throughout their lifespan, Like so, all living forms have something to depend on from their parental care. Nature defines this as a unique bondage, one must respect it.

Our sins have a way of punishing us, giving us sufficient time and warning, by ignoring it and continuing, the flame catches up and it can never get extinguished.

There are three ways of dealing with... Hurt, turn a deaf ear for all the hurt that others cause you or in an instant, pay back and retaliate them or choose to carry it with you for the rest of your life.

There is a certain approach to sanity, one can retain amidst turmoil and disturbances. Which has the roots of Maturity within. There is no need to go berserk, losing out all your energy.

To be an unlucky partner in marriage is like floating in empty space with no gravity, endless and relentless! If you are not tied up to a mothership, you are lost eternally in space.

It takes an insidious crafty
mind to discharge and disown
responsibility attached to self, failing
conditionally, when it's time to
reciprocate paying the debts of others,
The greed and avariciousness desecrates
the moral ethos of personality.

Everything has a character, and it is unique, we are remembered and identified by our character. Character is not acquired but congenitally blended, it is a complex matrix which never changes.

Living in time is not an easy thing, everything is time bound, certain good deeds need to be achieved in certain timeframes. Time lost can never be gained. We should learn to respect time and understand it's value.

When you hide your petty mind, however you try hard to expand the world, it shrinks!

Good memories live with us forever, what we have gained by our good deeds becomes our future moral codes, happiness reminders, contentment and satisfaction. We must keep doing good Karmas to enrich our own state of well-being.

What makes people say. Life is short? Yet, choose to live a miserable life? The poverty of mind haunts them, cunningness and selfishness to gain security surrounds them, their lives devotedly serve the pursuits of conceit and deceit.

Everything in life will pass, childhood to adulthood, hard times and happier times. Never attempt to dream anything permanent and hold on to it, for it can drown and suffocate you, complete your life cycle with memories.

The poor people look up at stars and wonder what it foretells, hoping for a change in their lives. The rich count their money for a richer life, the middle class count on both to survive. This is the tragedy of life.

The curses verily come home and
beat us down for the torments
we have inflicted on others. When we
suffer for our crimes, the cries are not
heard, the world becomes mute and
silent. Gods withdraw.

Some people can never accept love; they will never have trusted anyone and themselves. They distrust anything good. And believe that no good comes out from being good. They are impossible people.

Most of our miserable lives are because of gross human tendencies and dispositions, the world touched by greater concerns and humanity, moral and ethical behaviour can never go stinking and turns rotten.

Life convinces matured people to live in humility. Arrogant people not to live in pride, Ignorant people to live with wisdom. It never spares anyone till a lesson is learnt.

If you can amuse yourself by hurting, insulting and belittling others, not loving and caring, you have perfectly convinced yourself to be an incorrigible idiot.

An insensitive mind is immature, it laughs, mocks and shows sadistic tendencies. When serious confrontations challenge an insensitive mind, It buckles down like a ton of bricks.

Life has different hues and shades..pink for health, green for pastures, darker shades for difficulties and hardships. It never stays, and is not constant and permanent. It gets wiped away like the footprints on the sands.

Unlucky people are slated to expand their misfortune in marriage, money and property. Lucky people lift no finger, yet showered for untold fortunes.

'Characte' is not of the present, it is bequeathed by many births. I have seen it in good people!

The moment we start to isolate, look up at others differently, we get caught in a matrix of a vicious kind. When we can perceive others one amongst us, with needs, ambitions and hunger, we see ourselves in a different limelight.

All human relationships exist on a thin layer of ice, knowing it's depth and treading softly ensures safety or it drowns in ice cold waters. It is a delicate balanced approach in getting to know how not to offend, hurt other people.

Life can mould you the way it chooses. Use you like a pawn to make you a monk or a sinner by the time you ascend. Practice and cultivate humility, good faith and love, they can lead you well.

Our minds are our worst enemies. It can cause wars, distruction, famine, fear and apathy. We need to nourish it healthy! Purity of mind and sublime thoughts can open doors to happiness.

Your innate goodness must never become a commodity of trading. Never allow people to bargain, exploit and rule. Stand on firm grounds and be on Guard.

Anything you do to impress others crumbles down, things which you do to impress yourself succeeds.

Do not pray to God, for an extension of prosperity, thank him for his blessings, and pray for others welfare. Show indebtedness and gratitude.

Never be lost in pride and superiority and look down at people, all that you think you possess is not yours, it goes away in time. Show love and compassion, so you may get it back.

The intimate knowledge of people may shock you, never get to know, It is always better to know them, just enough to greet them. Good fences ensure good neighbors.

If an unborn were to have a fuller
idea of how life would be on earth,
they will resist their birth for sure!

Always rejoice in your pleasant memories, they are God's blessings, not the memories that frozened you once. Otherwise, life becomes a nightmare to live with. Dreams come to haunt you. Four seasons gives four reasons to believe that we can live, rejoice, and celebrate, to lead a pleasant life.

When arrows of deceit targets you, uncouth people bother, find ways to defend yourself and fight back. Invent survival techniques. It takes all kinds of circumstances to complete our life cycle.

Happiness is when you cheer up others, you cheer yourself up to be happy, find it in small things, live simple and make your life easy.

Every individual has self-respect and dignity, it is not required to fit into other's comfort zones! Life breeds several species, strong, weak and parasitic. Everyone takes on a niche of their own and lives.

$$F$$orgiving is all for the saints, it is an undesirable sacrifice, absurd and demoralising. You make others win by giving up your hurt and ego. When People do not spare a second chance for you, protect yourself.

Don't invite anger, jealousy and hate, to build nests in your head. Listen to the chirping of birds, observe nature and feel the breeze, let the divine feelings flow and fill your mind.

A ttitude is the first revelation, second is the humbleness, third is the action that marks a true gentleman.

Never match poor people with your money, they can give you love. Never attempt to buy them with your wealth, they are content with what they have already.

Our gratitude and indebtedness need to be aboundless, inexhaustible for mother nature. We are forever cradled by her immense resources and life supporting protection. We owe an equal responsibility to be respectful and committed towards nature. So we can pass on a beautiful world to our children.

Children are God's gift to us, their love, sense of belonging, and play enlivens us. Their world of innocence mocks our pride and prejudices. They are tiny harbingers of pristine purity for all our troubled existence.

Never lose faith in God, simply stretch your hand to seek in all your actions and deeds for survival. Never be distracted by non-believers, they never know their human limitations and living in arrogance, has perpetually blinded their vision.

When you have no desire, and pray for peaceful times, God knows what you want and supports you, when you avariciously ask him everything that you crave for, he takes away what you already have and give away to deserving people.

It is the insiders, who can hurt you most. They rightfully take everything from you for their selfish ends and drop you for a frivolous reason as if you mean nothing, sacrifices and hardships you suffered for them are overlooked and all forgotten.

O ne lifetime is enough, to know
that we must not have a second
chance in the pipeline to be born again.
For we know not how to live.

$$\mathbf{M}$$emories never leave us. It never tells you where you came from, what you are and where you are heading, It records your glory, misery and beats you every day with a hammer.

Every circumstance belonging to the present seemingly, is connected to a past as if it is mapped to perfection, the past rules your present, and the present rules your future. We are programmed till the software runs out, and the systems break down.

Never overstep the boundaries of universal spirit, disregard and live by spoilt ego. When the stakes are down, there will be none to care, wipe tears, Do not forget that somewhere there exists a boundary of discipline to accept.

Good fortune makes you arrogant, when you lose, and time runs out, you erase yourself in silence. When you recover, you become a true enlightened mortal.

Middle class liberal mind is a far superior victory over an upper class, miserly attitude towards life. The affluent appear to be a sick and ailing community with greed and avariciousness.

W hen you have enough wealth, spend on your comforts, never choose to exploit other people, and other people's resources, it is pure sin to be greedy and selfish. You neither fully enjoy what you possess nor you comfort your soul by gathering more abundance.

When you care for others in good faith, all the care bounces back to you. Love is what the world needs. A good human life not only keeps our lives pleasant and joyful but, we can carry it further into our afterlife.

When you carry a hammer in hand, every problem looks like a nail. Don't forget that nails can be uprooted by other means, the harder you hit, the deeper it goes inside or turns the other side. Focus on the problem and resolve it.

If your worst nightmare is too personal, you don't have to live with it! Redirect the devil to its grave.

There is no misfortune so repulsive that, when you take the disquieting attitude to burial grounds along with you. You enter a spirit world. The time to heal is now! and take only the good with you, at least other folks in the cemetery would greet you well.

When you look at an elderly person, firstly extend love, not arrogance, not neglect, but understanding. Attitude reveals who you are. After all, senior people will have lived their lifetime, and would have gained certain wisdom.

The best teacher in life is life
itself. When you grow old and
see other folks advancing in age, pride
melts down like a wax candle.

Count your blessings, be thankful to God. What does not belong to you, will never be yours. Never toil for what you cannot get. Find happiness within yourself.

Never construe a man as bad, seeing him today and judge him, recollect your memories of him from the past and count his goodness. If the goodness outweighs the bad, pardon him.

When you treat mean people reasonably well, you get back shades of gross behaviour one way or the other. Avoid them, never try to educate them, they are born special. Leave them alone.

Repentance is like a high tidal wave, beating on a turbulent ocean, with the rising full moon, guiding your emotions to subdue, renounce and surrender.

Overlook a defined enemy and be courteous to him, but never, a person who grew in your backyard and treats you inhuman, he is the worst of the lot!

Goodness observed in a child must not be construed as learning imparted by parents alone, it is a bequeathed legacy from the many previous births, qualities which have surfaced now giving a character.

When some actions are aimed towards the larger cause, and the impact is felt by all, there is an unprecedented aura of happiness surrounding us. However short run it may be, the effect compounds multiple times and appears eternal.

The greatest gift any parent could give a child is a happy childhood, good memories, joyful moments, rest is all synthetic concoctions.

Our lives are a journey with stops, transits and turns leading to nowhere, the only way we could undertake is God-realization. And in fulfilling our human birth by loving all living beings.

The best of minds retain innocence and recall moments of shared joy's, loving moments as unforgettable. The value of these memories becomes loftier against the mean circumstances, where just a few scratches would have appeared.

Happiness is a mirage, when you go near, it melts away, when you feel it is touching your skin, it slips away. Never chase happiness, you get it when it knocks on your door.

It is very obvious what we get from being negative, adhering to evil plans and machinations, it certainly does lead us to nowhere and through us on the rocks. We become so incapacitated we cannot rise up again to face the rest of our life.

The more people I meet, the more I subtract them. The residual numbers become so scant, that I wish I ought to sit on an isolated rock far away and endlessly look up at the horizon.

Fiercely guard your self-respect,
it is the only thing that leaves
you strong all your life.

It is astonishing why some people are so deprived, they replace all unpleasantness where pleasantness could bring them wonderful happiness. In place of love, they substitute hate, like to dislikes, pride to prejudices, such people never grow.

Good things become memories. Bad things accompany us as shadows. Both the good and bad, hit the rocks on rough seas to snatch our lives.

Your subconscious mind reflects your true self. Your dreams reflect your anxieties, nature and future. Isn't this a way to find out who you are?

Never be exploited by deceit, cunningness, dishonesty. Show them respite and neglect, do not feed the devil by your helplessness.

S ome show diplomacy, talk, hide,
do nothing. Relationship is what
relationship does, it is not lopsided but a
two way traffic!

Tough times are a real test of our strength. If we stretch it, we have goosebumps, if we shrink it, it wards off side effects!

Marriage is one strong stimulus that serves your karmic sentence. However hard you try, it takes a toll simply because you are caught in an inescapable net. It is compounded with two bags of karmic load seesawing left to right.

You know what you struggled to achieve, the price you paid, and what you got in turn. Don't be swayed by others' comments, look for affirmations and sympathies. For people who attempt to judge you, simply ask them if they have worn your shoes anytime?

When your guts and wellness becomes an eyesore for mean people. Kill them by your nonchalance without hard retaliation.

D espicable characters try to enslave people, to any extent to get their jobs done. They never look back even to thank you.

Sometimes in life, we have to revisit our childhood, to find innocence, laughter and frolic to overcome problems of adult life. Too much stress and strain are likely to destroy our health.

$$L$$ove..is a precious thing, always keep your doors open, allow it to sweep inside you, extend it to others. The time you withhold, the opportunity may not present itself again and would never come back.

$$W$$ith bipolar people, do not look for reasons, justice or morals. Do not partake in their misery, they are best left alone, they suffer their karma and you suffer yours.

When you think you know yourself well, never underestimate other's ability to know you better! Never be complacent. It opens new doors of awareness and enlightenment.

$$A$$n advanced mind silently observes the gross mind, and hides the shame with a thin smile, not responding to any reaction and response.

A blissful mind takes a break even when it's pushed to agitation and turbulence. It's calm disposition makes any disturbed mind come to its senses. Like the fragrance of lavender inducing sleep.

The worst behaviour hurled at you by others, convinces you of the existence of evil, Do not perpetuate and support it. Live life in appreciation of the good, erase all ill will without hurting others and move on.

For a person who has seen the high & low ebbs of life, nothing stays to bother. Detachment elevates him to higher planes and he converts bad times to compliment tough times.

Things which are not destined to come to us will never come, however hard we try. What has to come will break all precedents and fall on our lap.

Most of my happiness stemmed from my sincere prayers. The effects were so dramatic, that I never felt that I was alone.

We are not bound to each other, although we choose to live together, all of us have journeys of our own, we are strangers on a journey, we meet and part, relationships are just an arrangement.

Living with uncertain people is pure exhaustion, by partnering you will double your load of karma. Attitudes overshadow your independence, to avoid them you crawl inside a Cocoon and when the weather is good, refresh and step out.

One can retaliate an insult the very moment someone hurts or not retaliate and carry it for the rest of our life, you can heal an old hurt by recollecting an old instance with the person responsible and call him anything you like. But never carry with you and moan.

A life of regrets is a life not worth living, Right or wrong one should accept and never get disturbed. Disown defeatist tendency. Make your living robust and strong, fill it with positivity and good convictions.

Never regret the life you have lived, it was one which was destined, nothing could have changed it, either for better or worse, and made a difference!

I love good people and fall in love with them naturally. World is full of unpleasant people and they submerge you to the depths of their choice. Retain good people as they are simply precious.

$$\mathbf{W}$$e desire what we want, God gives us what we deserve, after all, he has loads of subjects to take care of!

You can never satisfy people whom you have to serve, their madness, obsessions are insatiable. They are forever hungry, infected with mental poverty and prevail as long as you provide.

Never get too close in relationships, small gaps in relationships help you to retain the essence, the closer you go, you invite trouble and sweat. An impulsive mind can trust even a story, of a tortoise carrying an elephant on its back.

Sometimes God chooses us to help others, without our least awareness, for he cannot appear before us, he has grand designs for everyone and he will see to it that it is carried forward from God's perspectives all are equal. He delivers what he wants.

Time to live is now, whatever you want to achieve you must attain in your prime age, live fully and completely in childhood, adolescence and in adulthood, later slow down, but never disqualify yourself, as you grow in your age, the joyous moments goes off.

When bad things happen to good people, it appears that God slept away those minutes unknowingly out of exhaustion and the temple bells froze in the distance!

To find peace, it is necessary to disengage certain connections, it isn't worth playing victim for too long. All things exist and impact, it is left to us to choose. Some relationships need bonding, some need to cease.

People who exhibit bad actions obviously, have a disquieting karma load, they may lessen it in time to come, we must give them time to heal. Leave them alone.

If you withhold an unspoken word of gratitude for the scare of reciprocation and commitment on your part, you evidently lose the status of uprightness!

Never make yourself the center of the universe, if you do you will be lost as a minute pebble on the beach, and you can do very little. If you collectively think for all living forms on earth, you could reach and transport yourself to any latitude.

$$B$$ est thing to cheer up oneself is to cheer up others, treat humanity as a whole single entity. Then in that instance, the world belongs to you.

When you are unhappy, it only declares that the world you expected isn't coming. Change the circumstances and align with it, you make hay, while the sun shines and feel better.

$$W$$hat can haunt us most in our after life, is the regression of not having given love for the discerning people. This vacuum can never be filled. The time we have now is precious, we must use it for positive causes.

T hose who spend a lifetime with us, deserve more than what we can give them!

L ove is the supreme food we can give and share it with others. Give it with sincerity and ungrudgingly.

The wars we create in our minds are enough to trigger storms, ignite grasslands, forests and to burn life forms. We must first extinguish the fire, evil forces within us.

Think of others, and do good. It bounces back to you multiple times. The power of goodness brightens your aura! Do not wait till you transcend to heaven or hell, there is both here on earth, you only have to choose wisely.

There is something about our brains; when you nurture it with good thoughts, it gives happiness, you pollute it, and it buries you deeper in the hell hole on earth!

Karmic sufferings are so vicious in some people that even if you try to help them they do not understand and reject you, stare at you with their blank look! Even to accept help and to ease load of karma they hesitate.

If I were to be complacent, adamant in my own beliefs, see no other alternate pathways and shut the doors forever, I see no future and roll in the muck, stuck in the quicksand and vanquish faster than I think. Beliefs, dogmas are all for a closed mind. Truth and realities all have expiry dates.

When you trust God, the power within you becomes so strong it can resist a storm. Counter any inimitable force of destiny, damage and devastate. Your form may look fragile but your will become impregnable.

Live with people who love you, never be a recipient alone, reciprocate, so that every ticking minute will belong to you!

The root cause of all suffering is the absence of love. All misunderstandings emanate from self-centered desires, discarding considerations and expectations of others in utter nonchalance and trying to make your position comfortable.

For some, bonding lasts till the adhesive lasts. A time served and ceased. Never to realize the advantage of human bondage, they forget their short escapades from their host like hit and run.

There cannot be a higher self persecution, than shutting out all doors of intellectual advancement, refusing, discording all that is good. This state of exile is insanity. Refusing to remain as a human being.

Time to be happy is now. Discard all frailties, liberate from selfishness, embrace a lasting world of joy and happiness. Chasing out a life of complexity, dilemma and self-denial. Do not lose this precious pulsating life of existence.

By our critics we learn who we are, not from those who praise us for advantage or gain.

One cannot live beyond genuine needs, illbegotton wealth and resources, it turns out to be a curse and burden, which you cannot happily carry with you, it is bad for the family, society and perpetuates sickness to humanity.

People who shy away at times of need and support for others, are cowards. They think they are safe and protected, certain of their life and not knowing a storm brewing round the corner, can uproot them.

A wise man's silence towards deception and cunningness is not to be construed as a sign of weakness, He stands a mute witness, for the future calamity that befalls. To teach a lesson in humility for the unmindful people.

Abuses and evil intent, that a mad man targets at you, makes him look a lesser mortal when he declares his insanity. You need to disconnect and seek a peaceful and tranquil place to remain calm.

When you share with others,
see to their comfort, get to
understand from other's viewpoint the
whole world opens doors for you, you
become a winner and share rewards
with them.

The influence of intellectual people rejuvenates at your cellular level, catching up with them and spending your time with them, you will experience a new birth.

G od hears your prayers, before you recite chants and mantras, he renews our faith by his presence and miracles. He does everything to see you are happy. We must show gratitude.

Sometimes, intelligent people find an excuse to slip away from stupid people, they are sensitive not because they should run, but because they know, that they can beat up and confuse them by their stupidity.

When God wants to change your life, he can snatch, add, multiple and dissolve without your consent outrightly. It is his will to fabricate, design and position you. We cannot grasp why he does it at times. After all, he knows what we deserve.

If I had ever dropped a person because he does not serve me anymore; I have lost a certain human dignity!

It is a lasting truth, that once you reject a relationship, it can never see a sunrise, however you try!

When your time of advantage ceases, pay back the donor the benefit of gratitude! Everything in life has a price to pay! Or else you remain in debt.

The price every man pays for his
life, carries substantial value; it
cannot be scaled down by any measure
by others.

The moment we understand the value of toil and sweat, we stop laughing at others, start respecting others!

Our mundane struggle for existence, the blueprint and design, geometrical space confines us without thresholds. Some expand their life and some shrink away.

Taking people for granted, and attempting to be in their private space, is an unthinkable trespassing, one should not do. Neither a parent or anyone else, for that matter, must refrain from doing it.

Human beings are God's seal on earth, his blessings are many, he gave life-sustaining gifts, sun, Moon, Air and Water, whatever he gave mankind is grossly misused, polluted and desecrated. Lessening his life span, inviting famine, disease and dying prematurely.

A wrong attitude is immutable, it alters everyone's chemistry by a mere dropping of a hat! Negative attitudes are largely intriguing and annoying, it doesn't serve anybody.

The price of restraint is a boon
for a gentle soul, it adorns men
of substance, makes them superior over
men of straw and ignorance.

If you separate from parents with ideological differences, and drop them like hot potatoes, you declare yourself as an imbecile, having no moral standing and would never ever have paid their debts.

Wealth gained serves just a lifetime. Character earned by good deeds gives you a fortune that serves you even in other existence.

The adjective Karma, good or bad, must not be used as a tool to persecute people against each other, to hurt, punish one another in times of misfortune. instead of consoling and wiping tears.

Battling with mundane things for a living, but in the inner sanctum I am at - God's feet, blissfully. Knowing that this life won't last long and will pass away.

Never damage a person's repute and dignity, friend or foe. You will lose him forever, give respect and do not shame him in public. You will scar your soul permanently!

If you are silent in the face of injustice, you are a victim trapped inside a coal mine without a life support!

Some marriages uplift life, some advance our Karma baggage, some take you to a battlefield, and some leave no trace of you.

Persecution of Children, harmless animals and nature, unleashes a satanic force which buries our soul into an abysmal hell. Instead substitute it with love and affection, Our advanced senses must prevail.

People who are unhappy in the present have the tendency to go back into the past, visit places where they lived, search for old buddies and subconsciously start a journey, literally in total recall. The need to acquire spiritual strength becomes an essential prerequisite.

People who know pain, and have suffered much, seek God and show indebtedness. They become loyal even to the slightest relief they receive, in their extended life, for they understand what life stands for.

If you create an awareness of decency in an unruly crowd, it is enough to bring them discipline, good behaviour demonstrated, can influence and bring out order in disorder.

$$\mathbf{B}$$ipolar people impose themselves on others, undermining the intelligence of others and get things done. They go crazy if their things are not met, all at the cost of other people's discomfort.

$$B$$ad influences on good people can be crippling, good influence on bad people at least can slow them down!

The righteous way of living is by taking ownership of one's own conscience, and keeping it good. Living humanely and in dignity.

Never rob off a childhood, chide children to meaningless disciplines, and watch over them suspiciously. Give them the liberty and teach them to be responsible. They will grow up promisingly.

A sick mind turns the whole world into a hellhole, for itself and others with no lateral outlets! It appears a safe haven to some, cannot come out stuck inside. Such unfortunate people die in shame and cast off their mortal coil like a snake shedding its skin.

The incorrigible people will never mutate, they never change, they will have convinced themselves to be perfect, they never budge. Never waste your time, just take a walk.

If as a parent if you do not have the courage to correct children when they take on to crossroads, then you should never have been a parent. This is unmistakably a crime you committed for the family.

Once the still waters are stirred, it dissolves all reflections, feelings, emotions and relationships which you can never regain! Handle good people with at most care, never lose them even by accident.

There are no predictable designs for our lives, we would never know even if they exist. We must live by our instincts, logic and intelligence alone, it is strategic management and optimisation of life.

The best period in life is when you can have a decent meal, peace of mind, respect, strength to pursue what you want, and be recognized for what you are.

The value of a thing is known only when you have lost it, good people are your backbone, if you break them you cannot get them back and you are cursed to be lonesome.

When we face the inescapable; firstly, God strengthens you, then empowers you with a will of your own. There is a tangential end, all things come to a halt and you will have redemption.

Few tear droplets on the grave earned is worth more than what we acquired and lived for in this life! Love... brought us here, with love we must depart.

There is an element of melancholic boredom in the way humans live, from birth to death, everyone recycling the same life pattern with some variants and with shades of difference.

In understanding the depth of sorrow, we make our roots stronger, spread our tentacles to resist future challenges.

Faith in God is a strong force, insurmountable difficulties eases out, as if it never existed. Hope keeps us alive.

Bad people are always in places, never hold a grudge and never attempt to change them! believe that God is a better judge and leave them alone.

All morals point out something we owe to others, to think for others and do good. Not to torture and to inflict pain.

R efined liars and cheats can
enact so well, they can cry in
gratitude and disappear before your
tears dry up!

Every soul craves for love and understanding, but very few give it to others and receive it!

It is the state of mind that needs to be healthy, love and empathy must find its place. More you give, the more you get. The rewards are immeasurable.

What comes out of a loving heart is an assurance and a message of purity, and what spills from the heartless are nothing short of wretchedness, cobwebs from the dry lands.

G od cares for children, bestowing them the magic of innocence, a fairy world of their own to forget and lose themselves in a dreamland at the bequest of misfortune.

If the devil in you, prompts you mean, the good in yourself should burn it, never to allow it to rise again!

Unknowingly we exhibit our culture, mind and learning by our conduct with others, some things we cannot hide! We tell what we are!

Silence observed and felt, acknowledges the presence of God in any place and time, rejuvenates our inner soul!

Elderly folks ask something beyond the ordinary, which costs you nothing, the greatest joy comes when you have given them love and affection in their lifetime.

The definition of insanity is repeating and beating the drums in a single note and expecting a symphony to be orchestrated.

Every pursuit of struggle, fought long may not lift you up, do not wait for the time to come, be the person you need to be.

The enduring words of kindness has many connotations, choose any form and let it touch other people, Never deny a single moment. Even those who do not deserve it will be waiting to receive it.

When you stand in a temple,
pray without expectations,
You take birth afresh and come under
the loving protection of God.

When your own people turn toxic, detoxifying them must be through some surgical means with no room for other procedures, like the appendix which has no distinct role in human anatomy, it should be removed.

Never overlook loving yourself.
It is just not a survival instinct,
it is everything you need on earth first
as a priority.

All actions are preceded by intentions, and bear specific connotations, if it is stretched with love and compassion reactions will be pleasant, Otherwise, it can desecrate the very purpose intentions.

Oftentimes, a closer introspection reveals the floating toxins within our minds, we need to purge it away and cleans it. If you allow it to accumulate it eats away all the living cells.

Butterflies live for a day winning a thousand hearts, humans live long to pursue intangibles and die in lonesome graves!

The Truth is that, there is no generation superior to another, the roots are the same, the green leaves just turn yellow. Every generation will have served their best, facing their circumstances.

Life is a big recycle bin, all the young and the old never escape the seasons of childhood, adulthood and senility. Lives of all mankind appear monotonous and are of the same textured material. We falsely claim that we are different and unique.

Time served in this existence is purely Karmic, good people leave a record having lived bad and good, and the worst people having lived well with no meanings attached and the ordinary people having lived in mediocrity with no difference. When the cycle ends, nobody remembers us.

The youthful days roll in pride & cheer, adulthood bears the overwhelming burden of responsibility, old age chases the mirage of love and happiness!

C hronic remorse is an undesirable factor, for all worries there is an end. We stretch it unnecessarily, it should not culminate into a habit, and snatch our happiness.

G ood people strengthen your faith, bad people weaken your faith. Cunning people destroy your faith! Never disown what you believe is good.

If you have earned love in the family, no one can reject you! The whole cosmos surrounds you with love.

Y`ou` are happiest when you see others being happy. Your subconscious state never allows you to be happy when others are unhappy.

If someone is making you miserable or making you happy, be certain that it is the previous Karmic repayments.

When we learn to let go of things that we are attached to, we attain liberation and gain equilibrium. Happiness is not about hoarding wealth, property and money. Happiness is what you share with others and relationships that you cherish.

You could be the meanest apple, but never prove it. Grow amongst all, at least it brings you. A certain awareness.

Live in boundaries of happiness,
small clusters of it optimized,
not in pursuit of total happiness, you
may not even make it to the borders.

Guilt and conscience can never be camouflaged, it shows off in multiple shades. Leaving stigmas forever to haunt.

When God is everything and is responsible for you, never be anxious of this existence, or the next!

The slimiest snake I have ever seen is the one which uses another snake for its own advantage! Beware of such a snake in your garden.

When in difficult times, a closed door opens as if pushed by the wind, and let's in a cool breeze of air, God gives you an opportunity to overcome hardships, he can in an instant shut the doors for you, never be upset, simply accept without contradictions.

One cannot live by ideologies, there is fluidity in adaptations and understanding, perceptions as we go on. We need to take life as it comes, finding truth at every step ahead.

When good people are praised and acknowledged, bad people watching them desire to attach themselves to good people with laurels, without greatness!

There is a certain speed which catches momentum in troubled times, sweeping you to the moments of relief! All these are acts of God.

Life can never be the same, We can not be complacent or feel down in dumps, or jump in ecstasy, life tides are not in our control. Submit yourself in humility!

When you have love and have given it from the depths, even the birds recall in the park, and ask why you didn't come for a walk if you are found missing.

'Ego' goes for a slumber, when life tides simmers down, howling like a lone wolf, it no longer can hurt anyone, and is shy of asking for help!

If you were selfish most of your life, if you ever ask a favour you go untrustworthy and folks invariably suspect you are in some game play, and you may not qualify for any favourable time. Build an image that you are worthy.

F orgiveness can be a great virtue,
practicing it may make one a
saint; but, it can never cement the sense
of loss and hurt, heal wounds and build a
bridge to cross

Emotions can overstep boundaries, negotiate unreasonably, and can cause deeper damage. Stand aloof from sentiments and negotiate.

The way to resolve a nagging issue is to use a bit of optimism, a bit of pragmatism and willingness to continue despite uncertain results!

The silence of good people will be heard by the Gods and they are protected. The schemes of bad people are devoured by demons and they are left high and dry.

Never feel sick of responsibility, when you have willingly accepted, you can never go low, sickness comes from avoiding the healthy burden and to start unreasonably negotiating with yourself.

Sufferings are not reserved for the poor alone, even the affluent suffer by their greed, due to isolation, helplessness and denial of love. There are different manifestations of poverty. Mental poverty is the foremost.

Mind is what you think, react and accept. Observation leads you to psychic abilities to unravel facts, and hidden motives. Inferences you make must be backed by intellect and fair judgment.

Humility is not submissiveness,
it is the first sign of greatness,
maturity and wholesomeness.

Jealous people are restless and disturbed, they perpetually undermine others to feel contented!

A crude uncut diamond gains it's value when it is cleaned and polished; don't be in a hurry to show your value, let it be seen at a pace and in layers, when it's time it shines on its own accord.

S ilence must be the first reaction
to an agitated assault, it propels
sanity within and makes them wonder if
they are truly human.

We get to know people, when we understand them, they are such a blend and so complex, no second person will be the same. It takes time to study, observe and to interpret before we can accept or reject them. It is scary meeting new people!

Something inexplicable happens when you converse with elderly folks, the affection they give rekindles all dying hopes! Their confidence against odds and resilience leaves a new sparkle in us. They narrate things in confidence.

Some people manipulate good people for their ends and dump them. They are possessed and the devil never seems to leave them, it keeps them busy. Once bitten twice shy; manipulative talent can never longlast, they meet dead ends soon.

Like an orphan child's tears cannot be wiped forever, the burden of memory will be conditioned. Given a new lease of life, they feel the comfort but with certain seriousness. Life cannot be wholesome happiness it has strings attached to it.

Life is a barefoot walk for all of us. Each blister dries up in the memory lane. We cannot walk the path on green grass always! The count of people who would say; living was a merry go round experience are very few, Most people would confide that enough is enough and would never look forward for a second birth.

D on't invite a cunning jackal for
a bite? It takes a greedy bite,
steps aside and leaves gently, comes
back for leftovers in herds.

Bad people always convince themselves and conceive, to further their views of righteousness focused on good people, their sin is their form of justice.

When your destiny leaves no option but to live with disquieting people, you evolve!

R ejoice in what God gives you,
rich or poor must never beg.
Show gratitude and live on. Nothing that
belongs to us today is forever ours!

The cause of unhappiness is expectations, having none is bliss. Contentment with whatever you have is happiness.

S ecret of happiness lies in bringing a smile on others' faces honestly, for it has a boomerang effect, leaving you totally joyful.

Selfishness can never ever overwhelm a craving mind, it leaves one inadequate and incomplete! anything you acquire, anything you earn does not fulfil your emptiness.

L ooking back at life, at times we feel it isn't worth a dime! We are a recycled species, struggle to exist, live on petty differences, have pride and prejudices. We do not evolve, increase our comforts and go back to earth.

Something is lost in time and space, if things meant for your happiness do not serve you, you compromise a life very different from what you aspired for. Your wealth becomes useless.

Never create a heaven on earth by acquiring more and more wealth, it won't last long; create abundance of love, help the needy, it enlivens you for a lifetime!

Wish we all could rein in emotional sufferings and focus on resolving issues of life, we must cast off all fears and become strong. The cause of all mortality is internal fears, anxieties which we call private and shut our doors.

If you fail to reason out with someone, neutralise by taking a walk, you could do something constructive, don't attempt to change people, It is none of your business!

F or your own precious well being - love and respect, reserve a portion of happiness to yourself. Never undermine this importance! If you are cheerful all things shine, if you laugh the whole world laughs.

A decent life is what matters most, rest is all that may come and may leave, external influences should not pull us down. Find peace and contentment!

If you study a man who is incorrigible closely, you will know why he is special. His profile would shock you even more than his temperament, behaviour and disposition.

A child's smile is a lot different than that of a grumpy adult, unconditional and healing! They are torchbearers of an unknown divine force for all our miseries and disturbed life.

N ever rush a child's growth, every ticking moment is so precious, time is an elixir for him to grow into a healthy, strong individual. His growing years must be with grandparents, don't ever deny it!

If God's ultimate aim is to create dharma & and make all of us chaste and peace loving, why does he not liberate us free from the clutches of karma and rebirth cycle? He could do a fast job.

What the elderly folks desire in old age, is truly a second childhood! They want attention and love, and a sense of belonging and laughter. Give them ungrudgingly. Happiness and joy will come as a spiritual advantage.

When we abstain from not knowing the cause of other's suffering, it becomes even more complex, compounded with fear and guilt. We should help people in genuine circumstances,

Never look at people at the cellular level, trojans, malwares, viruses attack you. Accept them as they are, if you need them. Never attempt to customize them.

When you believe in good faith and in the power of goodness, all that is maliciously threatening issues of life do not near you. Life goes on by God's grace!

Families must have values, deficiencies make it look unseemingly disquieting, forlorn and lost. The first human bondage you create leaves a wonderful precedent.

When the mind is conscious seeking loftier content it rejects the mundane and gross level substance! It opens up like a flower blooming in sunshine and spreading pleasant aroma.

We fight an endless battle in our stressful life, we struggle for existence and our health gives way, Relationships weaken for which we would have given our heart and soul, all that is earthly crumbles down.

Few would take steps towards God realisation.

All of us are modest about our secrets, things we cannot confide with others, we pretend we are happy, we never escape this vicious cycle till death do us part. Suffering humanity will never cease and cannot come out of this delusion.

An egoistic mind enjoys a momentary euphoric dream fulfilment when its pride finds a place, and buckles down, when it is out of place for it has no convictions of its own.

Over time, relationships die hard, because they are time serving, priorities and uneven desires become overwhelming. Relationships become the last of priorities, values wane and stagger. Human beings are essentially born selfish. We can see this evidently with everyone.

To overcome unpleasant moments, come out of it respectfully, not escaping but refusing to be a part of it, just walk away.

When God decides to lift you, he may use a combination of odd circumstances and unknown people, strangers could give you a helping hand, never stop to question. All these are his miracles.

If we could dump all our emotional garbage, we can become willing scavengers.

Keeping the debris for long stinks, it rots and maggots could attack. Our minds are our destiny, we must keep it neat and clean, devoid of all wasteful scrap materials.

Helping people in their time of suffering is an immense act of humanity, it awakens the 'Saint' in us. But with instances of extreme measure, with wicked people, who are submerged in darkness and ignorance, we can only pray.

What cannot be cured must be endured, we should know our limitations, Situations, people or nagging issues are best dealt with intelligence and patience.

Scheming, cunning people must never target a silent gentle soul, they are far beyond games people play, and observe with an eagle's eye they can easily identify bad intentions, malice, jealousy and prejudices.

Our lives are all too synthetic, each enacting a role, some keep it forever some lessen as they learn to disown. They come with different nature; the good, bad and the ugly, most people are without conscience and exceptional few, dedicate to serve humanity.

Focusing on elements with lasting values, we need stock up and practice to make our lives happy. All residual scrap elements cause pain and suffering. When we protect good things, the same goodness protects us.

$$\text{A}$$gony inflicted on others, rubs on us too, their pain and hurt experiences start to hover around people who are the cause for it. These people suffer, survive those agonizing moments and the effects will certainly cripple them in time.

If you are convinced that you are a good man, never be swayed by what others talk of you, conviction and faith shall be your armoury. If you watch a high breed dog accompanying his owner in the street, all street dogs bark in the distance.

Standing before God in a temple, I go blank, I never ask for anything, earthly expectations are volatile and transient. I would ask him only which stays permanently. a spiritual rebirth, in a spiritual realm.

"God willing" must be our mantra, to lay all our anxieties, frustrations and sufferings at his disposal and accept his will, material wealth what we earn can not support us in sickness and replace life. It satiates our fulfilment of pleasures.

Clouds gather in the skies, some rain on you, some shine on you, some float for you and some merely follow you. They exhibit certain relationships akin to human nature. Some people enlivens your life, some others make you shine and mediocre people make you miserable.

The tortoise lives to see many generations, the longest living creature. How is life treating them, how do they manage to live so long, what do they gain from living so long. Is it a curse or a boon? Maybe, we should learn it's secrets.

Sometimes, the inevitable relationships we endure, are being distanced by God, to break a certain undesirable connection and terminate. If he finds out one is happy and the other is unhappy, to protect one he takes off the other.

Never miss those wonderful moments with a child, they teach us many lessons we need to learn leading us to a higher education, any University can give. Oftentimes, they change our personality.

Our transient lives, moves on, inundated, stirred and staggered, to a grinding halt by death. Death leaves us many messages, lessons, responsibilities making us serious towards life.

When someone closer dies, a part of yourself dies too. It not only takes them away but buries the living in memories!

Never impose your attitude with the ferocity you are born with discording other's feelings! the world never revolves around you. You revolve with it.

The protection God gives us is invaluable, the protection we build is vulnerable and is insecure. Learn to be humble.

Contemplate God, you will not wither away like dry leaves in autumn, but blossom in all seasons in everlasting touch of magic!

Loving is a transcending opportunity, unconditional and spontaneous, time to and make others happy, it is a fleeting moment and won't come again.

It surprises me beyond my grasp. How snobs behave, they exhibit refined values, inordinately, they do not have an iota of humanity, empathy and understanding for others.

Never be complacent when you help others, God uses you to do certain errands to help others who are in trouble! He loves you as much, and appoints you to carry out an assignment.

Sometimes life appears to be a Tom & Jerry... show. The trials and tribulations we undergo in the pursuit of happiness!

Thank God, all past karma's end,
takes the storm away. Fresh
ones begin, by discretion you advance
or denigrate by failing again.

The moment you leave your false pride, you realise what humbleness can do for you, get to know and perceive the wisdom of ages, and start with a new lease of life.

Never impose your ideals on others, spare yourself the peace you deserve, it is vainglorious to attempt changing other people, each one of them are stuck in their whirlwind of karma.

The more people you meet, the more you need to understand them, they invariably possess different attitudes, some can be disturbing. Your chances of finding good people and the ratio can be abysmal.

Keeping uncouth people at a distance from one's life, does not mean that we have to harbour prejudices, and perpetuate them, it is just that you retain a lesser and moderate level of respect.

A diplomatic way of handling difficult people is to treat them that they are nothing, the more importance you give the more they become difficult. Shift your gaze from them and look away.

Love denied, respect lost, faith weakend all sink beneath the sea, it can never float back on top again, it settles down as sediments and lay on the bottom of the sea. We must Protect and secure our dignity and respect.

We must gain the innocence
of a child, true concern, love
for others, laughter and friendships, life
is oceanic and is a serious matter. We
can make it a bit easier by allowing a
child-like disposition, assuredly we can
live better!

G od helps us when our destiny is cruel, showing no mercy, when we ask him to intervene by calling him genuinely, he hears our voice wherever we are, in hell or heaven.

Enrich your mental health by restraining anger, frustrations and prejudices. We cannot hold on to circumstances which are not in our control, it is better to give up, and not to get upset and persecute ourselves.

The toughest character, for all I know, loaded with arrogance and pride, beneath the surface will be fragile and weak. They are the most melancholic, lonesome people, when you tap them gently, they cry in your arms.

L ife goes on with all our imperfections, emptiness, likes, dislikes, haterednes and selfishness, leaving no room for anything pleasant, The choice is voluntary and chosen by our free will. We never realise the truth, and therefore have no regret and repentance.

Even the best of weather, rains, snow and sunlight will have no effect on a troubled mind, polluted and spoiled. These are the ones who do not want to know that the world can be sweet, joyful and pleasant.

People who cannot accept change, suffer the most, for such people the world looks as they see, troubled and lost. Their nature is stagnant, abominable and incorrigible. They silently disappear with their own black magic.

Some hoard, save hard, earn by foul means, good life repels them, they are insecure and have mental poverty. Their wealth does not protect them, they die a lonesome death.

The child plays with God in the initial years, with parents in growing years, later, takes the impact of parents, teachers, friends and society, by then it learns what is expected and gradually distances people for what they are.

If karma gives birth to good people, it should take away bad people soon as well, for they must transcend or descend from the earth. But it so happens that the space on earth is never empty, it gets filled for there are no reservations.

Our miseries arise from self pity, and selfishness. We want all the good for ourselves, we do not want anything to worry us, we do not care about other people's concerns. Life is not about living for ourselves, life becomes holistic when we can include others' well being. When we liberate the 'Self' we are enlightened for universal happiness!

Some changes in life are predestined and some are our own inducements. What is possible, impossible can happen without our consent. Everyone will have contributed their best of efforts in their life, they will be what they are today.

More I see a child smile and frolic in front of me, the more I want to protect and ensure a life of happiness for him. The child takes birth and in his growing years will know the hardships, at least, let us spare him some happy memorable memories and leave the rest to his destiny.

Unreasonable people can not become reasonable all of a sudden, study their motives, their mindset drives them back to their old habits. There is something with their genes which do not favour dramatic changes.

Good people are humbled by harsh realities of life, for no fault of their own, missing something of life after a revival, they are driven back to isolation, some fight back to glory and some resign.

Like a log of wood on high seas, it continues to float and gather speed, we allow our destiny to go on in its journey, nothing can stop the forces, it is left to destiny to decide to take us to the shores or dump us somewhere else.

Your best friend is – Yourself. Take care, treat, be enthusiastic, be loving and gentle on your soul, before you land up searching another.

D eath alone can convince us of impermanence, but we live as immortals as long as we can.

A gross mind will never respect a lofty mind, it has its own submerged layers of adulteration which can never be cleansed. Never force an idea to a space where it cannot take, certain things fit the bill and where it belongs.

Anxieties of life do not cease, it is part of life, let it pass the tunnel it deems fit, chances are that it may become lighter in transit and lose its power and get diluted.

If all the struggles in life have made you stronger, never try to demonstrate your strength, conserve for the rest of your life and use it for a peaceful purpose. In senility what good is your strength?

If life were a certainty, a pursuit of happiness, we all would create a monumental record of living, mastering the art of living!

Finding happiness in small things
is contentment, a gratitude you
express for your maker. Not aspiring for
higher things which may outweigh your

When you refuse to learn what you do not know, you remain in ignorance. Which is a lifetime of curse. It is tough to manage without certain skills and to feel empty.

Marriage isn't a platform to celebrate Independence, it is about loving, sharing, supporting and honouring commitments, standing together in thick and thin circumstances without buckling down.

One cannot reconcile with toxic people, once bitten, twice shy. Keep away from them. If one cannot do good at least, do not make others' lives miserable.

We desecrate portions of earth, with our attitudes, temper and leave a legacy and depart. Too much debris gets filled, the next generation follows suit and further pollutes, more sickness, more scarcity and eventually die as a result. What kind of species are we?

Both good and bad people have opportunities, the good get help from others, the bad help themselves, both of them make a living.

Those who have suffered pain, loss and misfortune become humble disciples of God, those who are rich, proud and fortunate become arrogant, worship themselves.

If there were no punishment for crime, all would have gone to paradise. Paradise would have become one hell of a place.

N ever blame others for your life, you are the architect and the conductor of the orchestra called life, you are responsible for the design and fabrication. The material quality you use reflects your construction.

The biggest lessons we learn are from those, whom we have trusted most, and have turned their tables against us, years of trust and faith we had for them slips off, such a character is certainly of their own, selfishness corrupts them.

When you know you are wrong, and if your ego does not admit it, at least be a humble pie and follow what is right. And limit your participation. And make way for productive inflow, you will exist well.

One should never let go of people with beautiful minds. Our lives turn out to be enlivening and pulsating, it is a school of wisdom and great learning with no educational expense.

If we fail in our conscience, we can never find a moral equivalent. the mind cannot fill anything productive in its emptiness. We must retain a good conscience as we care for our health and good life.

Never compete with mean people, firstly you lose your generosity, secondly they will influence you so hard you will conserve every penny and make you hold on to it. The load becomes so much, you have to leave behind.

We must learn to live each day, for it won't return. Justify an earthly moment, sharing love with family, reserve time to pray to God.

W hen you have won a lifetime of battle, weapons used do not matter, it is that shield that made you formidable.

Uncertain Relationships work best, when it is kept in switch off and switch on modes, dormant and activated at times, not closing it forever. It permits us to mature.

If you succumb to the exploitation of any sort, you don't deserve to be human. Kill exploitation and live your life.

L ife is inundated with fear, anxiety and turmoil. The nature of our existence is to absorb all shocks and challenges and continue to lead a life of impermanence, rekindling the light of a formidable hope.

When I dislike someone for a reason, I change my chemistry so much that I can never be the same again.

My winnings, I felt an invisible power strengthened me, in failures, I realise it is the same power that halted me. God never stops loving me.

Why do we struggle to make life permanent when it is impermanent. We gain nothing, instead live life as it is.

Uncertain relationships work best when kept alive in switch off and switch on modes. It allows us to mature.

Few minutes spent in laughter, joy and understanding is more worthy of our entire life, than the advantage we get with the practice of pride and prejudices.

One cannot be self centered, enjoying life of comforts and looking for freebies. This syndrome is a mental sickness. This will solicit curses, disrepute and respite.

I am a theist, Big Bang theories do not convince me. It is humanly impossible even to believe that life is by accident.

When you reserve time for yourself, you see what your soul needs, serve it with all the care in the world. Whatever you had denied giving it, you serve a noble cause.

All living forms righteously have their own space and respect ungrudgingly. This must be honoured and reserved, nature welcomes this natural selection.

At the intervals of misfortune, one should prolong existence, if you truly deserve, god will handhold and lift you.

One single act of desecration on your part, can wipe out all the goodness that is expected of a relationship. Be honourable in all your life and till the end.

When you own a bad attitude, love to nurture its your look out and To keep it, but you have no moral right to heap it on others.

I have heard too much about forgiveness, but, I can never forgive, they become extinct to me, so my mind rests in peace.

Conflict arises when we fight for
ideologies. We must create our
own spaces, not to plant anything of ours
in others boundaries. Good fences...I
mean.

It looks like God wanted our lives
to be transient. Created us fragile,
flesh and blood. Sheltered us on earth,
insecure and helpless.

H umility is a virtue. It enhances
once stature, the more we
are, the more we step up our character.
Humility has the touch of the divine.

The moment you separate yourself, by self-interests, you blanket yourself in misery, live in a void and become sick. You continue to deprive others by not caring and supporting. You know only when you want them back.

Problems do not arise raking itself, it targets you only if you are unstable. Strengthen your spiritual being, build your defences.

When you trust God, you appreciate your life better, broaden your horizons.

In silence, you realise the truth, in speech you reach minds, in seeing you believe, but when you cry, you cry alone.

Testing moments must not steal our confidence and push us into emotional turmoil. We must construe it as a moment of challenge and stand up to it.

There is nothing we can do, we are not superhuman, beyond flesh and blood we cannot go further. God realisation and humility alone can keep us strong.

By constitution humans cannot contain overwhelming predicaments, God has to intervene at times. We are weak spiritually and stronger from outside.

A true worshiper has nothing to fear, nothing to lose and nothing to regret. God becomes the heart and soul of his devote.

Circumstantial wrongdoings appear human, intentional ones inhuman, all wrong doings stem from a disturbed mind. What goes on inside the mind must spring from chaste morals and ethics.

Karma doesn't show mercy even to newborns, it makes them cry, only to be silent when mothers pick them up. Which is the beginning.

$$\text{G}$$od wants to promote good souls. Hence, He snatches some lives with a short breath, only to separate good from the bad. For others he gives a long lease of life and observes them.

Nature somehow repays us in the same way we treat others, selfishness to deprived condition, good deeds to surprise gifts, mindless hurting others, to pure misery.

When you do good to people,
you add value to their lives,
infuse confidence, bounce them back to
life.

If you think by chasing money, you get richer. It may surprise you to know it won't. In sickness and loss of a loved one, the world looks at you from a distance.

Spiritual strength means; ability to operate in pristine purity of mind liberated and being in faith. It's a GOD experience.

It is not what destiny gave you to be, it is merely a program you lived. If you truly deserve there are higher portals of existence.

People who are dead remind us what we could have given them, and would have not given them; what we were supposed to have given. The birth reminds you what you could spare, with the elements of love.

Use strategies with cunning people, observe crafty people, oust freeloaders, freeze exploiters. Spare good people with your love and affection.

Attitude is the first revelation, second is the humbleness, third is the action that marks a true gentleman.

Hope keeps us. alive, faith
reassures us, the vision of God
and his invisible compassion is enough
to sustain and prolong our lives.

Never take life as if you own it, never be arrogant, you never know when the forces of life can humble you down. Lessons learnt in humility has lasting value.

Total surrender, unflinching faith can take us nearer to God, at times of great misfortune, when we can do nothing, we can use this faith alone to overcome our hardships.

One should never hinder the favours and blessings that destiny gives, allow the sunshine to fall inside your house in gratitude, you will have earned it without your awareness.

There exists an incomprehensible bond that sprouts instantly when we meet some people, it is certainly not of the present but have gained momentum from our previous births.

I realise God when I hear birds sing, when babies laugh, and elderly folks look happier and in contentment. We must support these acts of God to make this world a much happier place to live.

Something is lost, something is gained in life, when the term ends we leave behind every loss and gain in life, and in the transition cycle. what remains in memory is how much we were loved by others and how much we have loved others. This life is a battlefield, other soldiers play their part inevitably, nothing gained and nothing lost.

Like the raindrops on a blade of grass, unattached and not belonging, clear and transparent. Our minds can focus on God and ever be indebted.

When we fall, we realise the depth. When we claim, we realise our strength. Can we not realise God by looking up at the universe above?

We use just a fraction of our lives to love others, we become obsessed with the self, lose out on time to get rid of bad attitudes and do not heal.

9 798885 304658